The Most Beautiful Child

Story Debjani Chatterjee   *Pictures* Biman Mullick

CAMBRIDGE
UNIVERSITY PRESS

The Lakshmi owl stared at the goddess with unblinking eyes. The owl thought that Lakshmi, the goddess of wealth and good fortune, was the kindest and the loveliest of the goddesses in Heaven. Precious stones and wonderful jewels sparkled on her hair and body. The owl adored her and was very proud to be her pet.

The owl often served as Lakshmi's eyes and ears.
She told the goddess all the news of Heaven and Earth.
She would carry messages and help her in many little ways.

Sometimes the owl would change her size and become a giant bird. Then Lakshmi would climb on her back and the owl would fly the goddess wherever she wanted to go.

One day, Lakshmi was sitting in her garden, enjoying the cool breeze blowing through the perfumed flowers. The owl watched her from a nearby tree. She never tired of looking at the goddess. Lakshmi had removed a shining gold necklace from her throat and was playfully twirling it around her fingers. She was silent and thoughtful.

The owl wondered what the goddess was doing, so she flew down and sat on Lakshmi's knee. "Tell me, Goddess Lakshmi," she begged, "why have you taken off that beautiful necklace? What will you do with it?"

"Why, my pet," the goddess replied, "I was thinking that I would like to give this necklace to someone very special."

"Who to?" asked the owl. "Who will you give it to, Goddess Lakshmi? Who will be the lucky person?" She shifted her weight from one foot to the other and her head swayed from side to side. She knew that the goddess often gave gold and silver jewellery to people on Earth.

The goddess answered, smiling, "Yes, that is the very question I've been asking myself."

"And who have you decided on?" asked the owl. "Who? Who?" She nudged Lakshmi's hand with her feathery white head.

"Well," said Lakshmi, "as it's a most beautiful necklace, I have decided it should belong to the most beautiful child of all."

"Who? Who?" asked the owl, shaking her head and blinking in her impatience. "Who is that lucky one? Who is the most beautiful child? Who? Who?"

"You will decide that for me, my friend," said the smiling goddess. "Take this necklace and fly around the universe. Look and find out who is the most beautiful child of all. Put this around their neck. I know that you will make the right choice."

Carefully, the owl held the necklace in her beak
and flew away on this important duty.

The Lakshmi owl circled over the gardens, lakes and palaces of Heaven. She flew over the mountains, across the rivers, and down the green valleys, looking at every child of Heaven.

Then she flew to Earth. Her round eyes peered through the window of every home and school.

She stared through the cabin windows of ships.

She stared through the thick glass windows of aeroplanes.
She looked at all the children of every country on Earth.

Several days passed before the owl returned to her mistress. "Goddess Lakshmi, I am back," said the bird. She fluffed her snowy white feathers. "I have done as you asked. I looked at all the children on Earth and in Heaven. I gave your precious necklace to the most beautiful of all."

"Well done, my pet!" said Lakshmi, clapping her hands. "Tell me, was it difficult to make your choice? Who is the most beautiful child of all?"

"It was the easiest task in the world, Goddess Lakshmi," replied the owl, without blinking an eyelid. "I peeped into every home and looked at every single child.

But though there are many sweet and lovely children,
there was really no choice at all. None of them could match
my own little owlet. The most beautiful child of all is my baby,
fast asleep in our nest. I have given the necklace to her."

The goddess laughed and stretched out her lovely arms.
The Lakshmi owl spread its wings, and then she flew towards
the goddess.

Lakshmi stroked the owl's feathers lovingly and said,
"Yes, you have done very well. You have made the right
choice.

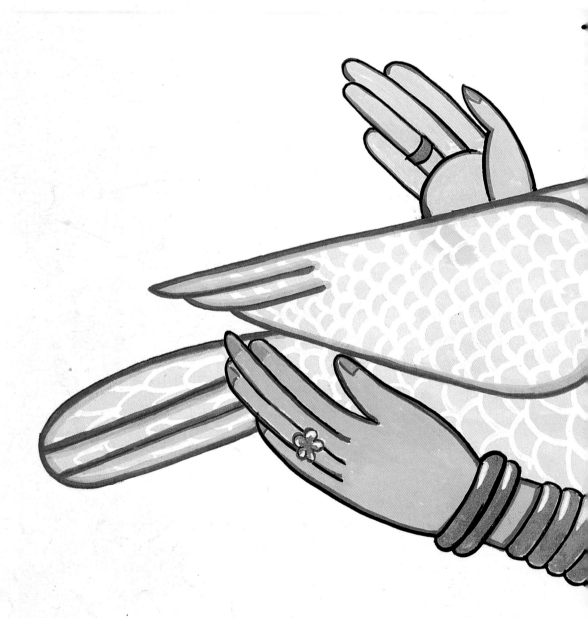

In every mother's eyes, her own child is the most beautiful of all!"